fun with art

Helen Webster

ARCTURUS

This edition published in 2009 by Arcturus Publishing Limited
26/27 Bickels Yard, 151–153 Bermondsey Street,
London SE1 3HA

Copyright © 2009 Arcturus Publishing Limited

ISBN: 978-1-84837-152-1

Author: Helen Webster
Editors: Rebecca Panayiotou and Fiona Tulloch
Text designer: Viki Ottewill
Additional design: Trevor Cook
Cover design: Zoe Mellors

Printed in Singapore

Contents

Contents

Using Colour

Craft and Collage

How to Paint

Introduction

If you sometimes wish you knew a bit more about drawing, painting or making fantastic arty things then this is the book for you! Covering things like mixing colours, drawing in perspective and using materials together, you'll be shown all the basics you need to make brilliant finished artworks. Below are some of the materials you will need to make the projects in this book. You might find you have quite a few of them at home without even realising it!

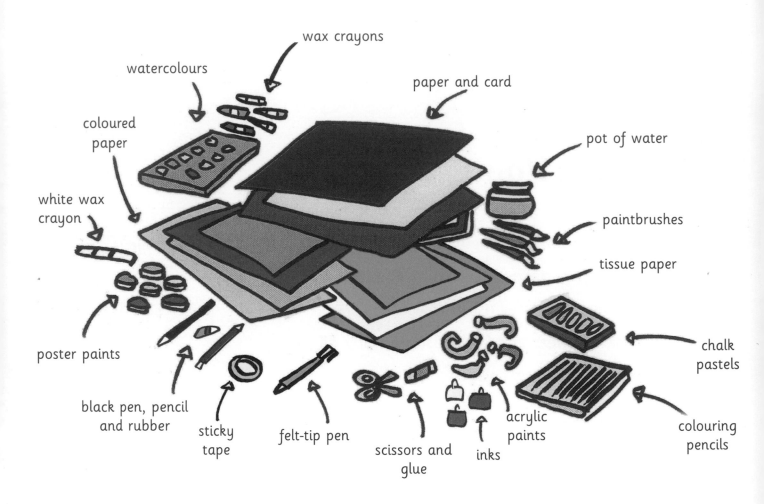

You'll learn how to use everyday art materials in totally new ways, such as how to get a soft swirly effect from felt-tip pens and how to use crayons to create a brilliant underwater effect. There's inspiration for making gifts, greeting cards and other things with the personal touch. It's a jam-packed, easy-to-follow guide that will show you how to really have fun with art!

Tips and Tricks

How to draw the easy way

To start off, we're going to show you an easy way to draw by using building blocks. We're going to demonstrate with animals.

Draw each step shown and see how you 'build' the shapes. Notice how it's not until stage 4 or 5 that they look like different animals!

You will need:

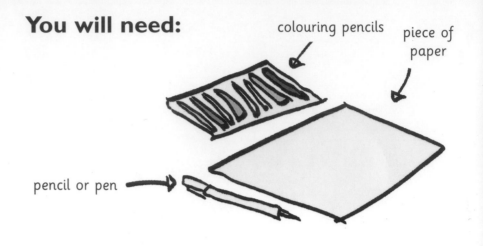

colouring pencils

piece of paper

pencil or pen

See how the detail is added in step 3. You then have two animal options – a mouse or a rabbit!

big round ears

long ribbed tail

long ears

short tail

1

2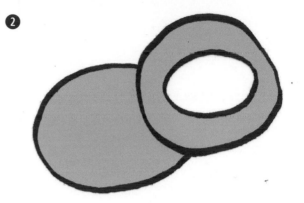

3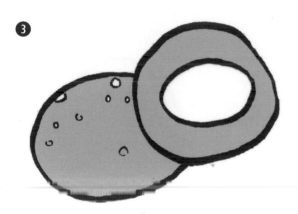

4

Will it be a pig or a reindeer? You decide!

5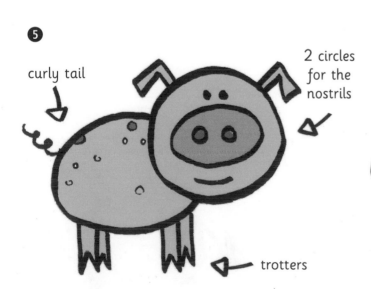

curly tail

2 circles for the nostrils

trotters

6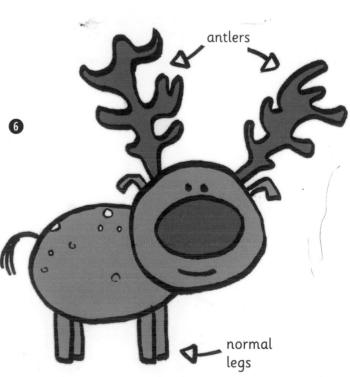

antlers

normal legs

9

How to draw using the playdough technique

Another way to draw animals is called the 'playdough technique' and it's very easy. Again, we're going to show you with animals. Every animal starts off as two balls of playdough stuck on top of each other.

You will need:

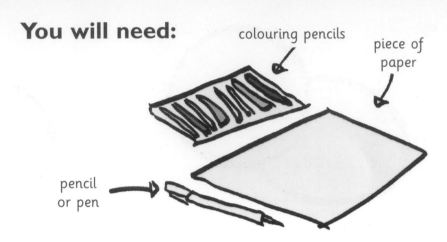

colouring pencils

piece of paper

pencil or pen

To demonstrate, we'll show you two ways to draw a dog – either standing on two legs, or on all fours. First let's look at a dog standing on two legs:

❶ Draw two 'playdough' balls on top of each other.

❷ Draw two feet at the bottom of your figure. They look like little paddles.

❸ Now add the arms and ears. You'll notice that they are exactly the same shape.

❹ Draw an upside down triangle for a nose and a pointy tail between the arm and leg.

❺ It's up to you to add your own fur markings and the expression on the face.

Now let's look at the dog on all fours:

❶ Again, draw your two doughballs, this time side by side.

❷ Draw the same two paddles at the bottom of the body.

❸ Add another pair of legs and some ears.

❹ The curved tail goes in the top left-hand corner.

❺ Again, add any final touches you like and you have yourself a brilliant, tail-wagging dog!

How to draw an object from an angle

So far we've been drawing objects from the side or face on. But what about drawing an object from an angle? Let's take a big tractor. We'll show you how to draw it from an interesting angle.

You will need:

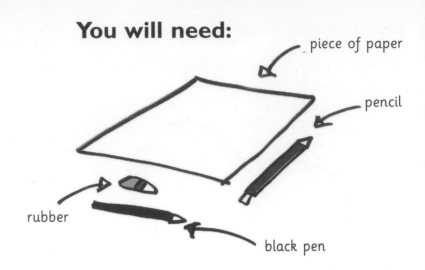

piece of paper

pencil

rubber

black pen

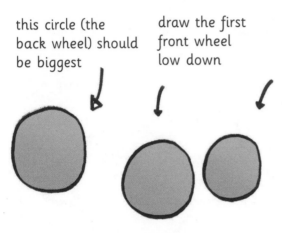

this circle (the back wheel) should be biggest

draw the first front wheel low down

this circle is smaller to make the second front wheel look further away

❶ Draw three circles to make the wheels. Look carefully at the position and size of each of the circles.

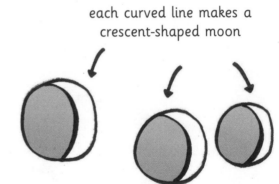

each curved line makes a crescent-shaped moon

❷ Now draw a curved line in each of your circles to give your wheels their 3D shape.

now the wheels look like doughnuts!

❸ To make the hubcaps, draw a smaller circle inside each wheel.

tractor body

❹ Next draw the body of the tractor. To start, try drawing a vertical line from top to bottom in between two of the wheels as shown above.

❺ Draw two lines to connect the front wheels. Now draw the bonnet above the lines as shown on the right. This is the hardest part so it might take a few attempts to get it right.

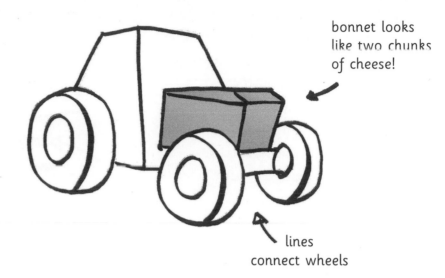

bonnet looks like two chunks of cheese!

lines connect wheels

❻ The tractor tyres need good tread – you can make this by drawing lots of little sausages! When you've done that, add a little circle and a curved line inside the two left wheels.

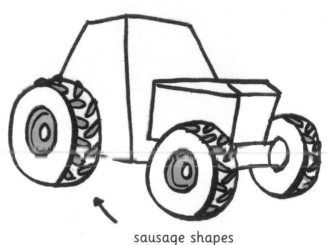

sausage shapes form tyre tread

❼ To finish off, add some windows and a black rectangle for an engine grill. Then colour in your farmyard masterpiece!

How to draw an object coming towards you

Now that you know how to draw an object from the side, it's time to learn how to draw something coming straight at you. We've chosen a truck! Remember that the colours we've used here are just to show you which piece to draw – don't colour in your picture until the end.

You will need:

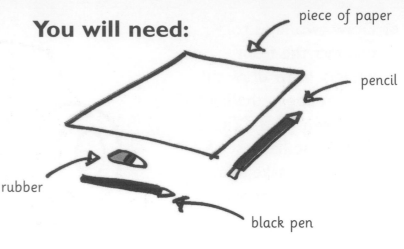

piece of paper

pencil

rubber

black pen

❶ Start by drawing a hexagon as shown.

❷ Put a sausage shape along the bottom to make a bumper.

bonnet

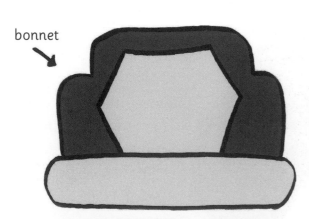

❸ Draw a curvy shape around your hexagon – it will look a bit like an armchair but it's really the bonnet.

hill shape

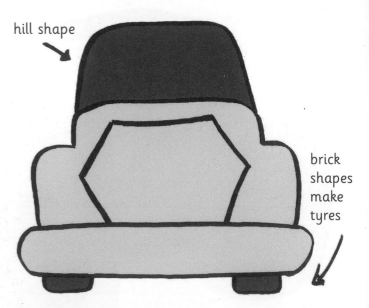

brick shapes make tyres

❹ On top of the bonnet, draw a kind of flat-topped hill. Then draw two brick shapes under the bumper.

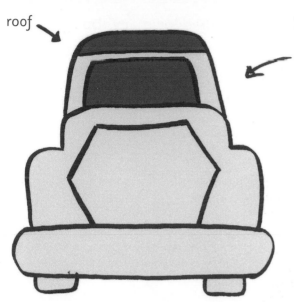

roof

windscreen

three semi-circles make lights for the top

two circles make bumper lights

❺ Put a smaller flat-topped hill inside the bigger one to make the windscreen. Draw a horizontal line just above this to make a roof.

❻ Use circles and semi-circles to make lights as shown. Put a smaller hexagon inside the big one and draw lots of lines across it to make an engine grill.

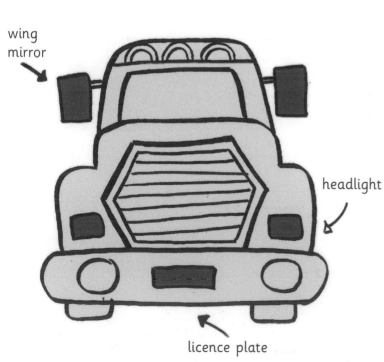

wing mirror

headlight

licence plate

❼ Now add five rectangles – two for wing mirrors, two for head beams and one to make a licence plate.

❽ We've coloured in the truck to make it look like a fire engine. Move out of the way!

15

How to use colours

To create an effective painting it is useful to know about colours. First of all, it's always helpful to learn about the three primary colours.

These are called 'primary' because no other colours can be mixed together to make them. Yellow, red and blue are the building blocks of most paintings.

primary colours

You can have lots of fun mixing primary colours together. When you do this, the resulting colour is called a secondary colour.

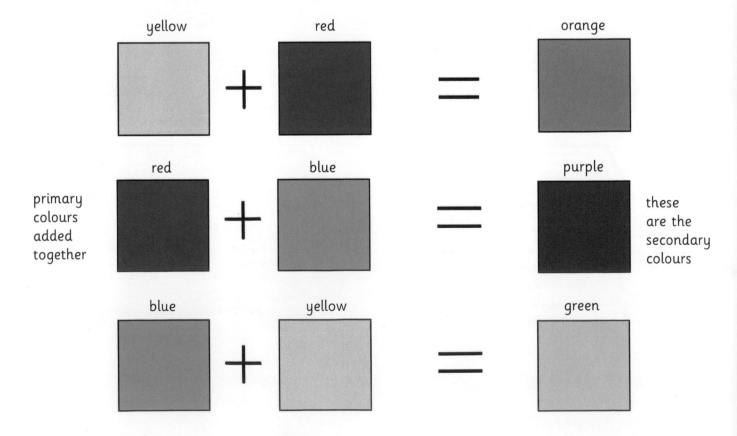

yellow		red		orange
+		=		

primary colours added together

red		blue		purple

these are the secondary colours

blue		yellow		green

When painting, you might sometimes want to refer to something called a 'colour wheel'. A colour wheel firstly helps you see what colours are complementary (these are the ones sitting opposite each other on the wheel) and secondly, it highlights harmonious colours. (These are the ones that are lying next to each other on the wheel.)

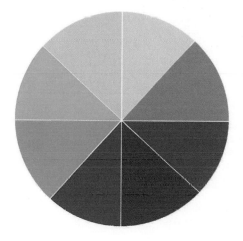

the colours that sit directly opposite each other on the colour wheel are called the complementary colours. This is because they work well when put together

these are the complementary colours

Another thing to take into account when painting is the colour tone. This can make the difference between a vivid strong picture and a subtle pale picture. Changing the tone can change the whole atmosphere of the picture.

light

dark

The tone of a colour is determined by how light or dark it is. You can change the tone by adding white to your paint or by making the paint more runny with water. (If you are using oil paints you will need to add oil paint thinner instead of water.)

How to use harmonious colours

We are now going to investigate the different effects you can create by mixing the primary colours.

When painting in shades of colour made from yellow and red, you find that the picture has an overall effect of looking strong and bright.

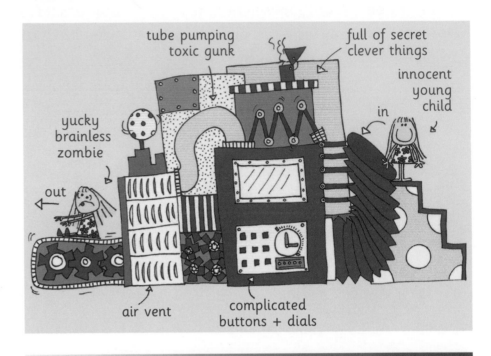

yellow   red

When painting in shades of colour made from red and blue, you will find that the picture has an overall effect of looking warm and rich.

red   blue

When painting in shades of colour made from blue and yellow, you will find that the picture has an overall effect of looking cool and fresh.

blue   yellow

When you experiment mixing all three primary colours, you get a rainbow of colours, which gives you more choice and a never-ending range of effects.

mixture of all 3 primary colours

Which painting do you prefer?

How to use shadows and shading

When drawing or painting it's very handy to know about different shades and where to put shadows. First of all you have to think about where the light is coming from.

The rule about shading is that the further away an object is from the light source, the darker the shade should be.

As for shadows, where we put them in our painting will depend on the direction of the light, as can be seen on the opposite page.

light source

notice how the brown shade gets darker the further away the floor is from the light source. The same applies to the wall and the bowl

have a really dark shadow underneath anything that touches the floor

try to make the shadow vaguely echo the shape of its figure

Look at this picture to see how different light sources create different shadows.

light C would create shadow C

light B would create shadow B

light D would create shadow D

light A would create shadow A

light E would create shadow E

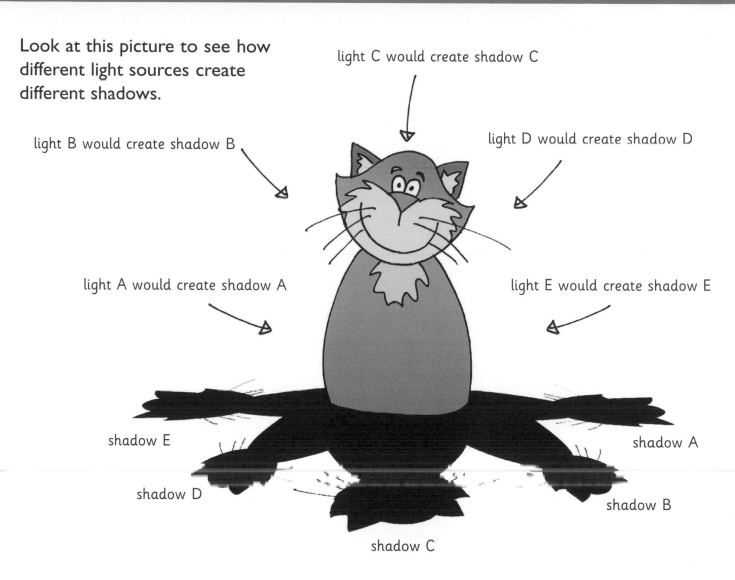

shadow E

shadow A

shadow D

shadow B

shadow C

So if the light was coming from here, where would the shadow be?

Would the tail be a lighter shade of orange than the head?

Where would the darkest shades be?

How to paint in perspective using watercolours

You will need:

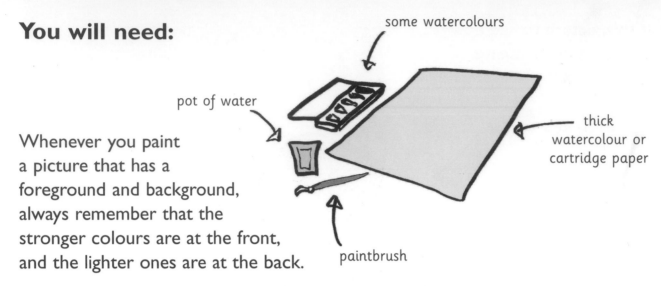

some watercolours

pot of water

thick watercolour or cartridge paper

paintbrush

Whenever you paint a picture that has a foreground and background, always remember that the stronger colours are at the front, and the lighter ones are at the back.

This landscape is a perfect example. Start with the furthest away subject first — in this case it's the sky. Paint this in a pale pinky purple colour.

always sketch the picture in pencil first

Paint the mountains in blue. As they get nearer you should use darker and darker blue.

wet each section before you paint it

5

if it's not
dark enough,
go over
it again

6

The closest mountain and the castle should be the strongest
blue and will have the most detail.

There you
go! Now
you know
how to
paint in
perspective!

How to get the most from colouring pencils

You will need:

lots of colouring pencils

a piece of paper

felt-tip pen or pencil

Colouring pencils are brilliant. You can use them in lots of different ways and they're really good for layering colour upon colour – just like we've done here with this cat!

First of all, let's have a look at a few colouring techniques you might want to use in your artwork:

cross-hatching different colours over each other

doing zig-zags over a flat colour

spiralling circles on top of each other

flat shading

layering with harmonious colours

strong shading of different colours on top of each other

Now let's put these techniques into practice in a picture!

1 Draw an image in pen or pencil. If you like, you can copy this crooked house on the right.

2 Now colour in all of the picture quickly and lightly. You want as much of the page covered as possible. This is so that you know roughly where the different colours are going to go.

3 Next, start on the biggest and most complicated part of the picture – in this case it's the roof. Once you get to this stage, you can start to use the different colouring techniques we've just looked at. For the roof, we're going to use strong shades of different colours on top of each other. This creates depth.

4 Once the roof is done, colour each item in the picture one by one: first the wood, then the grass and sprawling plant, then the pathway, and finally the sky.

5 The rich blue sky was achieved by cross-hatching. It's a really easy technique to do and immediately adds depth and texture to a picture.

How to use lots of art materials in one scene

For each of the colourful pictures in this book, we've used either colouring pencils, chalk pastels, acrylic paints, watercolours, poster paints or inks.

But what about using some of these different colouring materials together in one picture?

Let's experiment!

You will need:

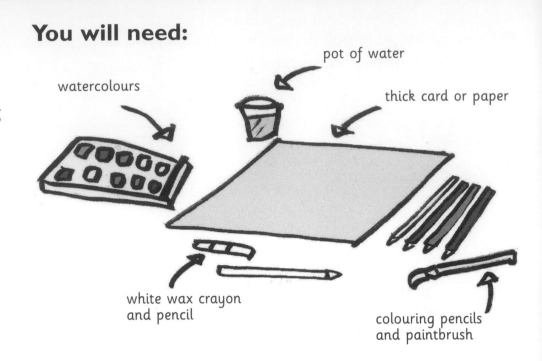

watercolours

pot of water

thick card or paper

white wax crayon and pencil

colouring pencils and paintbrush

❶ Take a piece of thick card or watercolour paper and make a rough pencil drawing of your scene. Don't forget the sheep – their bodies are like fluffy little clouds.

❷ Use a white wax crayon to go over the parts of the picture that you want to stay white. We've used a crayon for the steam billowing out of the train's funnel and for the sheep's fleeces.

3 Use a green watercolour to paint the field in front of your train. Don't worry about going around all the sheep as the paint will glide over their waxy backs.

4 Use brown watercolour paint for the brick wall around the tunnel – you can brush right over the steam and once again, the wax will stay white.

5 Now use a lighter green watercolour to paint the back field. Remember that using a paler shade, makes things look further away.

6 Choose a red watercolour to paint your steam train. Now turn to the next page of this book to find out how to finish off your great work of art.

Finishing touches to add to your scene

❼ Use any other watercolours you have to fill in the rest of your picture as shown. When your picture is dry, take out your colouring pencils and use them to add more detail. Draw some little green squiggles in the fields to make blades of grass. Then draw some panels on the train using a red pencil.

❽ Use a black colouring pencil to give each sheep a head and some stick legs. Now use your other pencils to shade over the rest of your picture – use colours that match the paint.

How to Draw

How to draw a cat using circles, triangles and sausages!

You will need:

Sometimes, when drawing an animal, it's handy to break down the animal's figure into different shapes. We're going to draw a cat using circles, triangles and sausages. This is a bit more advanced than the playdough technique from page 10.

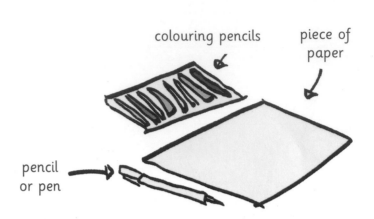

colouring pencils

piece of paper

pencil or pen

❶ Draw a circle.

❷ Now draw four small triangles on the edge of the circle as shown.

❸ A final triangle, which forms the nose, goes upside down in the centre of the circle.

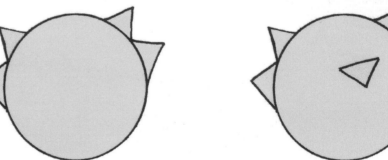

❹ Next draw a large semi-circle for the cat's body.

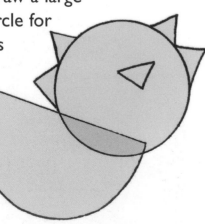

❺ The feet are also semi-circles – very small ones that have the flat edge facing downwards.

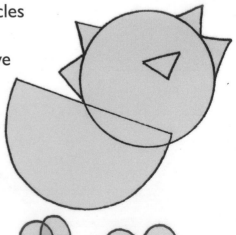

6 Now draw six curved lines for the whiskers and join the body and feet together with sausage-like legs.

7 The tail is also a long curly sausage!

8 To finish off, simply add two circles for the eyes, some raised eyebrows, zig-zags for the ear tufts, and a small mouth. Add any markings that you want on the fur.

How to draw easy peasy crocodiles

You will need:

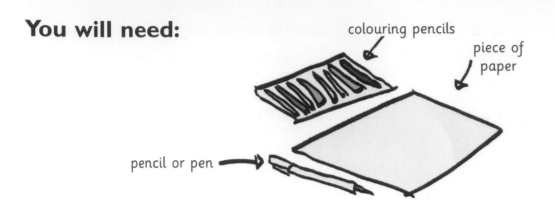

colouring pencils

piece of paper

pencil or pen

You'll impress all of your friends at school when you whip out your pencil and draw a cartoon crocodile, quick as a flash!

❶ The first stage is to draw two lines that should look like a hair grip, lying on its side.

❷ To form the mouth, simply draw a sideways 'V'.

draw a V on its side

❸ You're now ready to join the mouth to the body and add four sets of little stick legs.

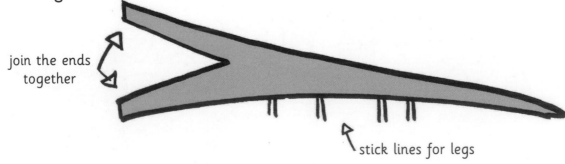

join the ends together

stick lines for legs

❹ Now we need lots and lots of little zig-zags! Fill the mouth with teeth and add lots of zig-zags to the crocodile's back, right to the end of his tail.

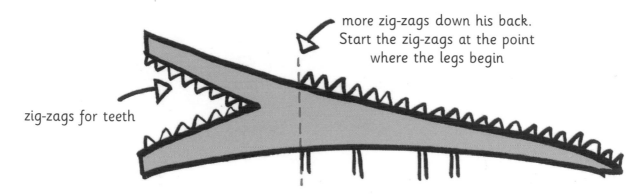

more zig-zags down his back. Start the zig-zags at the point where the legs begin

zig-zags for teeth

❺ Finally, draw four little sausages at the ends of the legs for the feet and give your croc some eyes. Hey presto! You've made yourself a cartoon crocodile!

The eyes are two dots inside circles. Place them just before the first zig-zag

finish the legs

Once you've got the hang of it, you'll be able to draw a crocodile from any shaped line. Just remember to follow the five simple steps!

How to draw a truck using simple shapes

A truck is easy to draw using lines, rectangles, squares and circles.

In each of the steps, the part of the picture you need to draw is shaded brown – but don't colour in your own picture until you have finished drawing it.

You will need:

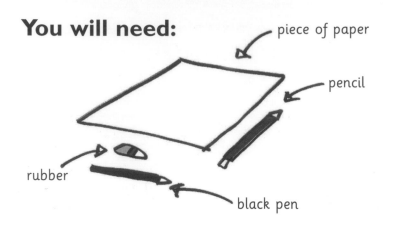

piece of paper

pencil

rubber

black pen

horizontal line

❶ Using a pencil or pen, draw a horizontal line.

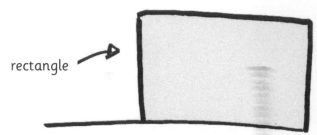

rectangle

❷ Put a rectangle on top of the line as shown to make the body of the truck.

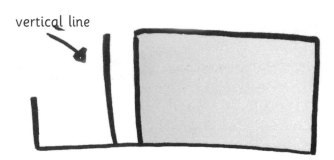

vertical line

❸ Draw two vertical lines – make one the same height as your rectangle and the other half as tall.

step shape

❹ Add three more lines to make a kind of step shape as shown. Now your truck has a cabin!

❺ Along the bottom of your truck, draw a long thin rectangle with three semi-circles cut out of it – one semi-circle should be under the cabin and two under the body.

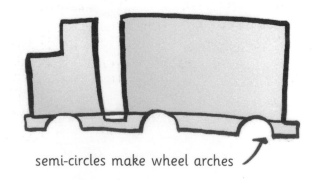

semi-circles make wheel arches

circle

6 Now draw a circle under each of the wheel arches to make the wheels.

7 Draw a smaller circle inside each of the big circles to make hubcaps.

smaller circle

square

8 Draw a square in the truck's cabin to make a window.

You can colour in your truck however you want. You'll be finished in a flash!

How to draw a cartoon dinosaur

You will need:

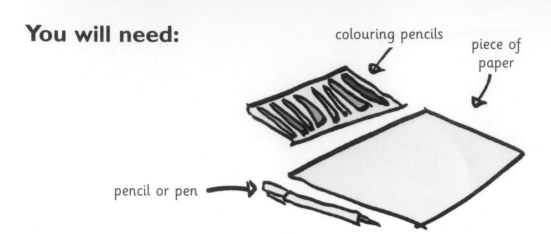

colouring pencils

piece of paper

pencil or pen

We are now going to show you how to draw a dinosaur!

❶ The building blocks of a dinosaur are its body and head, and these are made up of two eggs – or squished circles.

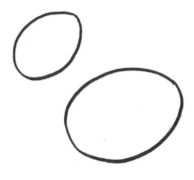

❷ Now join up the two eggs with a curved line and add a curved tail. The tail should be the same length as the head and the body.

curved line

the curved tail is as long as the head and the body

❸ Add two extra lines to complete the dinosaur's neck and tail.

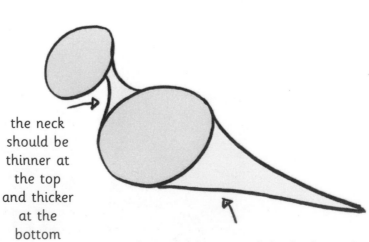

the neck should be thinner at the top and thicker at the bottom

join from the bottom of the body to the end of the tail

4 The eyes go at the top of the head, between two small sausage ears. The arms and legs are very simple. Just follow the diagram and the four easy steps!

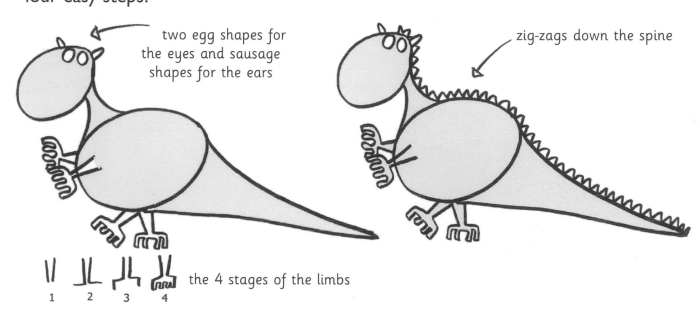

two egg shapes for the eyes and sausage shapes for the ears

the 4 stages of the limbs

1   2   3   4

5 Now draw a long line of zig-zags, starting at the top of the dinosaur's head and going right down to the bottom of his tail.

zig-zags down the spine

6 If you've drawn the outline in pencil, you can now go over the finished drawing with a pen. Just rub out the pencil marks and, left behind, you have a perfectly drawn dinosaur!

On the next page you can find out how to turn a dinosaur into a dragon!

How to turn a dinosaur into a dragon

If you can draw a dinosaur then you can draw a dragon. There are four things that you add to a dinosaur to turn it into a dragon:

Start from this stage (see page 37)

❶ **Wings** These should start at the point where the dinosaur's neck meets its body.

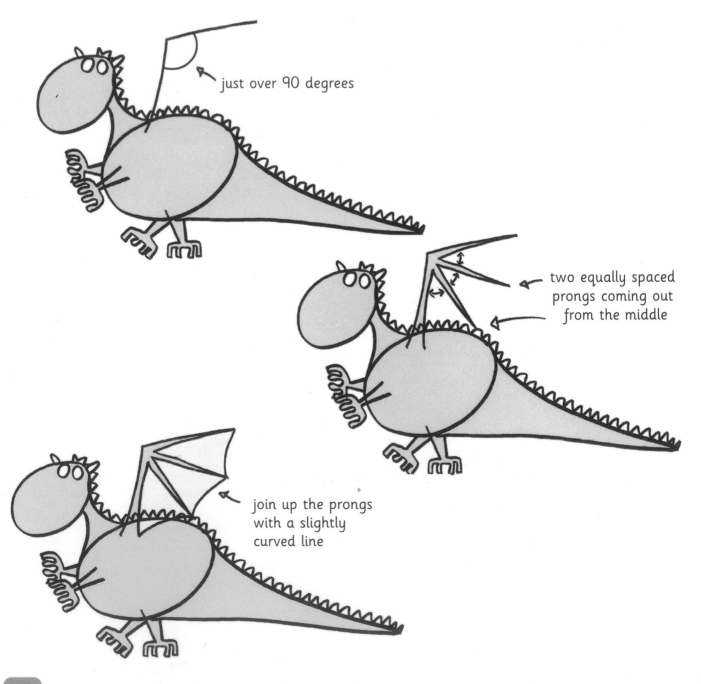

just over 90 degrees

two equally spaced prongs coming out from the middle

join up the prongs with a slightly curved line

2 **Fiery flames** Dragons can breathe fire! You have two choices here. You can either give your dinosaur a closed mouth and simply draw some nostrils with smoke wafting from them, or you can make him look really exciting with his mouth open, with hot fire coming out. It's up to you!

3 **Scales** A dragon has scaly skin. If you want, you can draw scales all over the body, but it sometimes looks more effective to draw just a few on the underbelly.

4 **Pointy tail** Add a triangle to make his tail pointed.

to make the dragon breathe fire, draw a triangle in the fat end of his head, add zig-zags for the teeth and wiggly swirls for the flames

to suggest the scales, draw some little 'u's over the belly area

place a triangle at the end of the pointed tail

How to draw a digger

A digger looks as if it could grab anything with its pincers — just like a crab!

You will need:

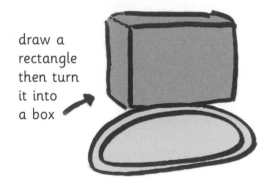

piece of paper

pencil

rubber

black pen

❶ Make a tyre by drawing a shape that looks like a squashed ring.

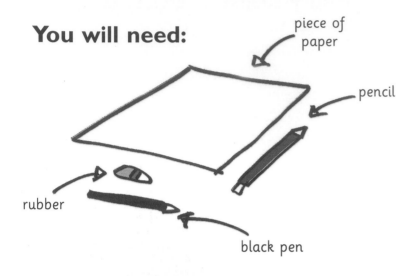

draw a rectangle then turn it into a box

❷ Draw a box shape to make the digger's cabin.

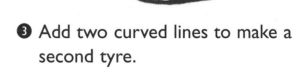

lines should follow curve of first tyre

❸ Add two curved lines to make a second tyre.

the last section of the digger's arm should be pointed

❹ Draw the digger's arm in three sections — start with the section that's attached to the cabin. Make the next section smaller and the third one smaller still.

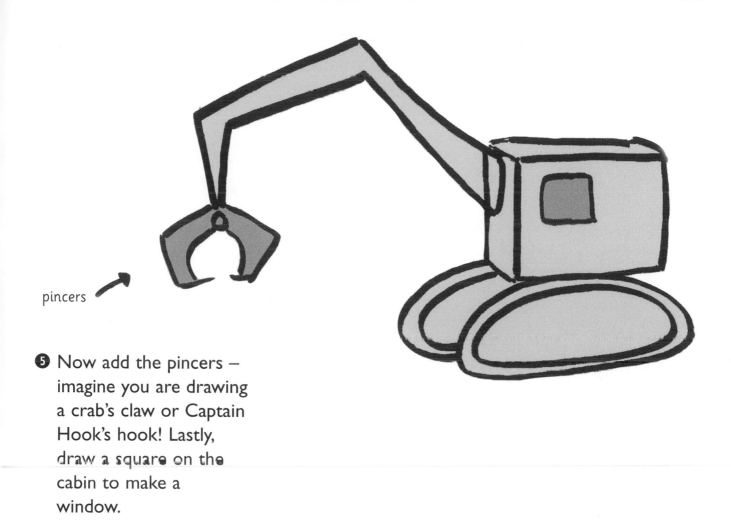

pincers

5 Now add the pincers — imagine you are drawing a crab's claw or Captain Hook's hook! Lastly, draw a square on the cabin to make a window.

6 Add a bit of colour and your finished digger is ready for action.

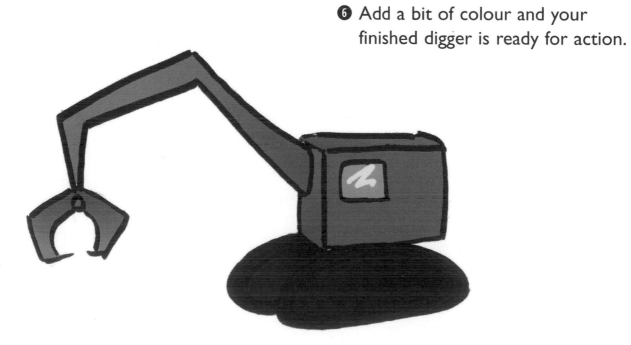

How to draw a steam train

Steam trains aren't as hard to draw as you might think.
Follow these steps and your train will soon be whistling!

You will need:

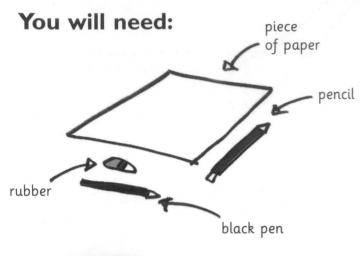

piece of paper

pencil

rubber

black pen

❶ Start with some wheels – draw two identical circles close together.

❷ To make the driver's cab, draw three sides of a tall rectangle on top of the wheel on the left as shown.

❸ Draw a long rectangle shape as shown to make the body – leave a curve in it where it meets the other wheel.

❹ Steam trains need to be cleaned inside – so add a curve to make a dome-shaped door and use a tiny rectangle for a handle.

❺ Draw two little circles to the right of your big circles to make front wheels. Now add two arch-shaped windows to the cab.

❻ Draw three rectangles along the top of your train. Put some small circles inside all the wheels then connect the front wheels to the train using little rectangles and lines as shown on the left.

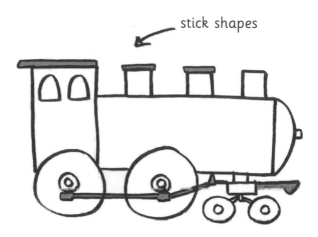

stick shapes

❼ Draw some rods to link the wheels together as shown in the picture on the right. Then draw three thin stick shapes along the top of the train.

steam dome

steam funnel

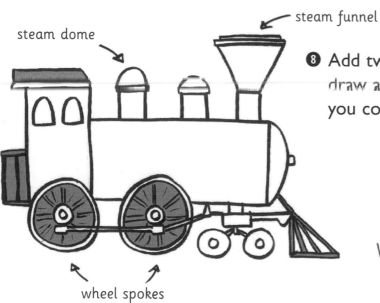

wheel spokes

❽ Add two semi-circles for steam domes and draw a big steam funnel. Some extra details you could add are shaded in green.

❾ Add a bell, some steam and anything else you can think of, then your train will be ready to go running down the track.

How to draw an enormous elephant

You will need:

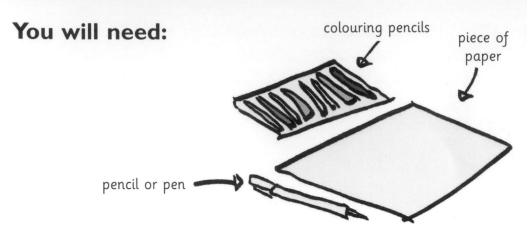

colouring pencils

piece of paper

pencil or pen

An elephant is made up of a rainbow, three boxes, three circles and a banana! Once you've learnt where they go, you can draw an elephant again and again.

❶ Let's start with the rainbow arc – the body. This arc should be fairly big and just a little to the left of your page.

the rainbow arc

❷ Now draw three boxes at the bottom of the arc. When you join them up you can make out where the legs are.

draw three boxes to make the legs

❸ The biggest and most important circle is the head. Put this on the right-hand side or, if you want the elephant to look directly at you, in the centre.

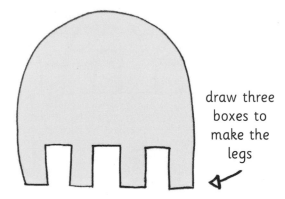

❹ For the ears, place two smaller circles either side of the head.

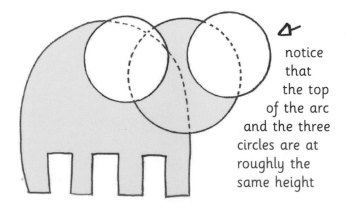

notice that the top of the arc and the three circles are at roughly the same height

❺ The trunk is easy peasy. Just imagine a long banana with a letter 'V' at the end. Voila!

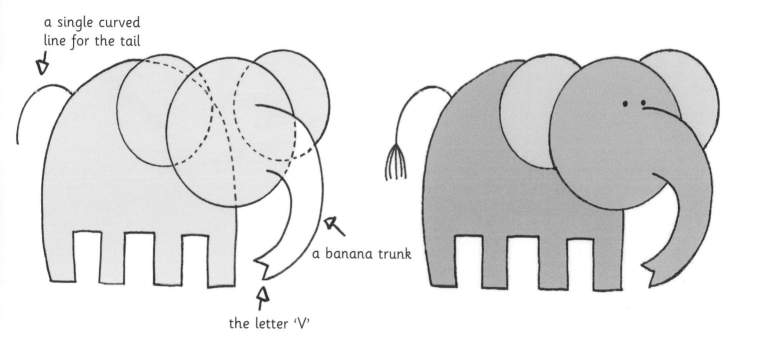

a single curved line for the tail

a banana trunk

the letter 'V'

❻ Why not draw a whole herd...in different colours!

How to draw a terrific tractor

Now let's draw a terrific tractor. In each of the steps below, the part of the picture you need to draw is shaded blue – but don't colour in your own picture until the end.

You will need:

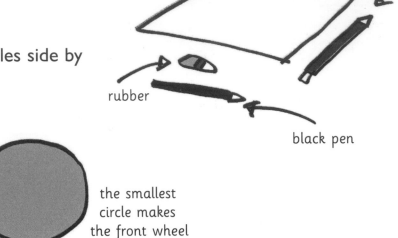

piece of paper

pencil

rubber

black pen

1 Draw two different-size circles side by side to make wheels.

the smallest circle makes the front wheel

straight lines drawn at different angles make the shape of the tractor's body

2 Copy the picture on the right to draw the body of your tractor – try drawing a straight line to join the wheels first.

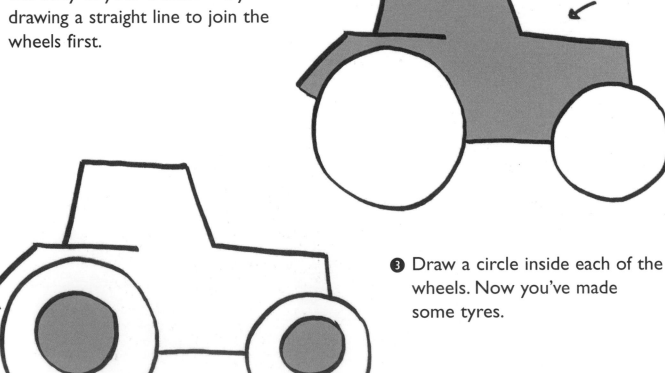

3 Draw a circle inside each of the wheels. Now you've made some tyres.

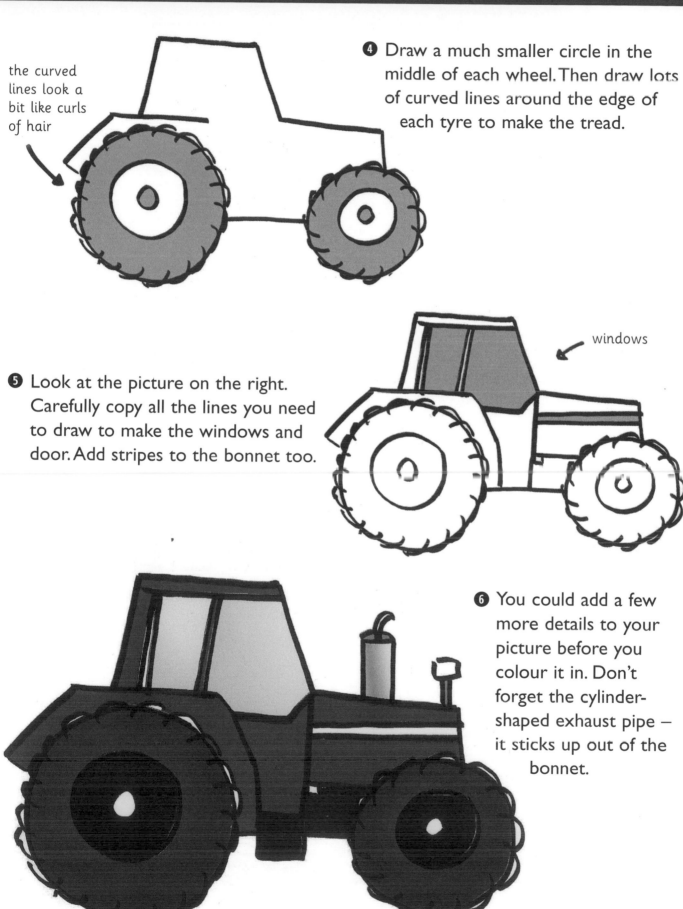

the curved lines look a bit like curls of hair

4 Draw a much smaller circle in the middle of each wheel. Then draw lots of curved lines around the edge of each tyre to make the tread.

windows

5 Look at the picture on the right. Carefully copy all the lines you need to draw to make the windows and door. Add stripes to the bonnet too.

6 You could add a few more details to your picture before you colour it in. Don't forget the cylinder-shaped exhaust pipe – it sticks up out of the bonnet.

How to draw today's trains

Drawing a modern train is a bit like drawing a truck. It's made up of lots of rectangles and circles. Let's start with an ordinary passenger train then look at how we can turn this into lots of different types of train.

You will need:

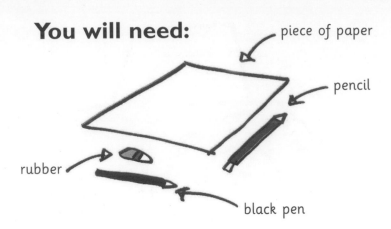

piece of paper

pencil

rubber

black pen

❶ Draw a long rectangle. Now draw three pairs of circles along the bottom to make wheels.

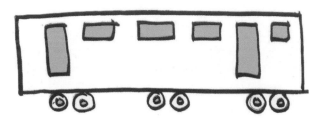

❷ Put a smaller circle inside each of the circles you've already drawn. Add some little rectangles to make windows and doors.

❸ Your train won't be going anywhere without the driver's carriage. This time, instead of drawing a rectangle, draw a more curvy shape like this one.

curvy nose

draw a connector so you can add your carriage to the back

you could draw the doors down to the floor

Let's whizz on to drawing high-speed trains.

make this end into a pointed-nose shape so your train looks super-fast

draw the wheels higher up so they are set into the body of your train

48

Trains carry all kinds of loads in different types of containers – here are some you could draw.

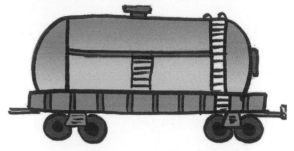

draw a giant sausage to make a cylinder-shaped tank

pile lots of thin rectangles on top of each other to make planks of timber – the straps holding them on look like long skinny fingers

draw a curvy line above a rectangle to make a heap of gravel – add lots of tiny circles for the little stones

draw patterns on a rectangle like this to turn a carriage into a food container

make a mail truck by drawing an envelope and a stamp on your rectangle instead

to draw a busy train, put some people in the windows – draw stick people if you want. Colour in all your trains before the guard blows the whistle!

How to draw a manic monkey

Now let's draw a monkey using the playdough technique you learned on page 10.

You will need:

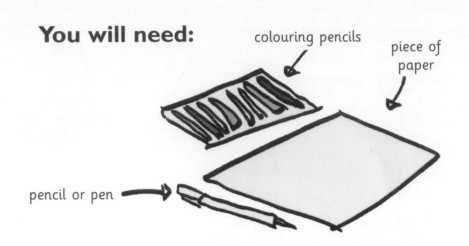

colouring pencils

piece of paper

pencil or pen

❶ First draw your two doughballs to form the head and body.

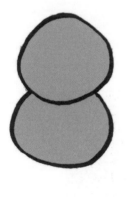

❷ Add the legs.

❸ Now add the arms.

❹ Give your monkey some ears and a tail.

❺ Draw a smaller circle on the monkey's head for a face.

❻ Now simply add the monkey's facial features and colour him in. Very cute!

Follow exactly the same steps to draw a monkey on all fours:

1 Again, draw your two doughballs.

2 Add two long, gangly legs.

3 Add some arms at an angle away from the body.

4 Draw a curly tail and add the ears either side of his head.

5 The face is a smaller circle in the centre of the head. Finally, give your monkey a cheesy grin!

How to draw two more trucks

On these pages you can find out how to draw a fire engine and a dumper truck. Let's start with the fire engine.

You will need:

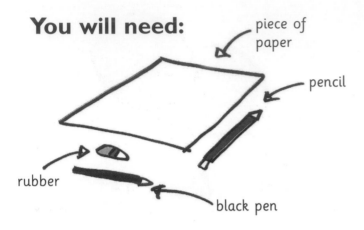

piece of paper

pencil

rubber

black pen

2 Now add some shading. This will give depth and texture. Make the lines very light at first – if you aren't happy with the shape, you can rub out the lines without leaving too many marks. Ink over your final sketch with a black pen.

1 Draw two circles for wheels. Copy the cab and body you can see in the picture below. To make the sky lift, sit a triangle on top of the body then add two diagonal lines. Draw a square dangling from the top.

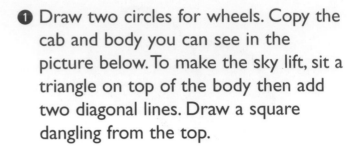
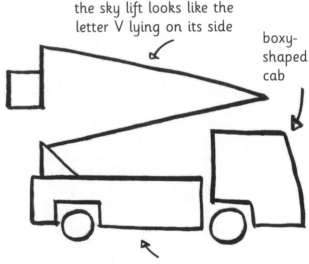

the sky lift looks like the letter V lying on its side

boxy-shaped cab

the body should be half as tall as the cab

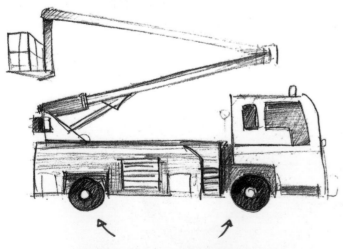

shade some parts more than others to make them darker

3 Paint your fire engine in a bright colour – but only in red of course!

A dumper truck has a very distinctive shape.

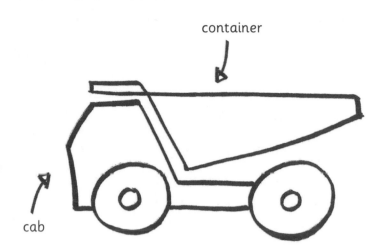

container

cab

❶ Start by drawing two wheels and link them together with a horizontal line. Finish off the cab shape as shown on the right. Now add the container – see if you can draw it without taking your pencil off the page!

making the rubble is a bit like drawing a cloud

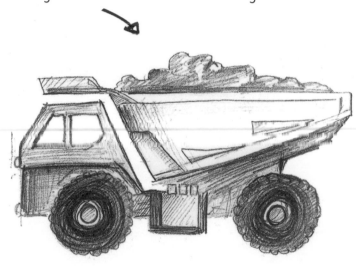

❷ Make some rubble by drawing a line with lots of curves in it. Next draw some windows on your cab. Add a few more details as shown to make your dumper truck even more realistic and adding more depth. Ink over it with a black pen when you are happy.

❸ Paint your finished dumper truck in orange or yellow – these trucks like to get noticed!

How to draw: summary

You can put together all the skills you've learned in this chapter to make one big scene. Create your own fun animal picture featuring a crocodile, a family of elephants, a few manic monkeys – even a dragon!

Now you've got the skills to produce great drawings, learn all about the best ways to colour your artworks in the next section. There's much more to art than just pens and pencils!

Using Colour

How to make a moving truck using pastels

Like colouring pencils, pastels are easy to draw with but you can also blend and layer the colours a bit like you can when you use paints. Here's a good introduction to using them.

You will need:

thick coloured paper

chalk pastels

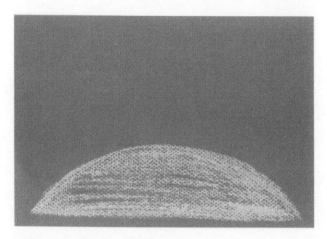

❶ Take a bright yellow pastel and draw a large semi-circle to make a hill shape. Now shade it in.

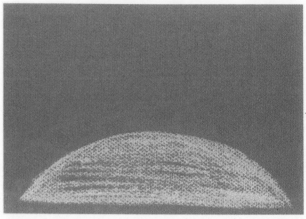

❷ Using a blue pastel, draw six little circles above the hill shape as shown. These are the wheels of the truck.

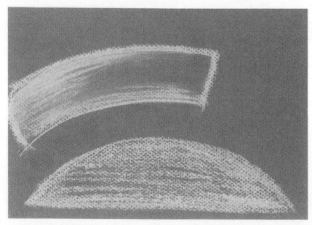

❸ Now take a lighter blue to give your truck a curved body as shown. Smudge the colour at the back of the truck with your finger.

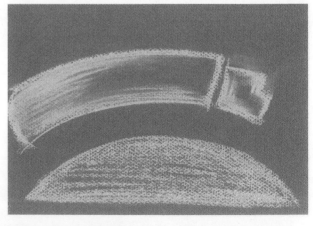

❹ Use the light blue to draw the cab. Look back at pages 34 and 35 if you need to practise drawing the cab. Then smudge the colour as before.

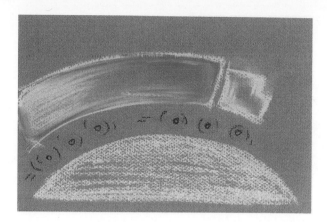

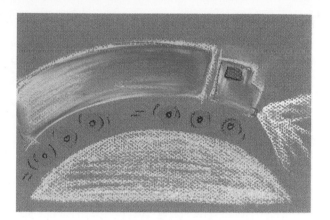

⑤ Take a black pastel and draw a small circle inside each wheel. Add some little curves around the wheels so they look like they are moving. Outline the truck's body in purple then smudge in the colour at the front using your thumb.

⑥ Do the same with the truck's cab. Now use a darker blue pastel for the cab window. To make the headlight beams, draw some rough lines in front of your truck using a white pastel. Then add a few more lines using a yellow.

⑦ Now go over the outline of the truck again with black and add a bit more shading as shown. It looks like it's on the move!

How to create a swirly lizard using felt-tip pens

You will need:

rubber

pencil

different coloured felt-tip pens

a piece of coloured paper

For the next picture we're going to draw a prehistoric lizard.

❶ Draw your lizard using a pink felt-tip pen. The one we've drawn is very similar to the crocodile from page 32, except that we've given it a humped back and a curled tail. (If you're not quite sure of the shape you're going to draw, draw it in pencil first and then go over it with your felt-tips.) Next, use a blue pen to draw some bubbly clouds.

❷ Get your pink felt-tip again and colour in the spine on the lizard's back as well as his legs. Now fill the body with lots and lots of little circles. Then, with the same pen, fill every circle with a tiny dot. Use a blue felt-tip pen to fill the clouds with lots of spiral 'shells'.

58

❸ Now use a green felt-tip to draw the grass as shown here.

❹ With an orange felt-tip pen, fill the sky with swirling lines that wrap around the clouds and lizard.

❺ It's time to go back to the lizard. With your pink felt-tip, draw circles around the small circles, and more circles around the bigger circles, until all the space is filled!

And there you have it…a very swirly-looking ancient lizard. A felt-tip masterpiece!

How to do a scratch resistance painting

You will need:

black ink

black pen

wax crayons: red, blue and yellow

a big paintbrush and a screwdriver or key

a piece of card or thick paper

❶ Draw out your name in block capitals. Make sure that all the letters are quite close to each other.

❷ Go round the outline of your name with a black pen, so that it is turned into one big shape.

❸ Use your red and blue wax crayons to colour in the letters.

❹ Add in a yellow crayoned background.

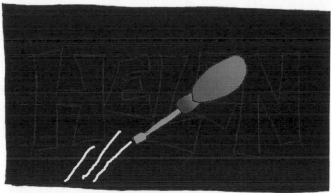

5 Now take your black ink and a big brush and paint over the whole image. Let the ink dry.

6 Using a screwdriver or a key, scrape enough ink away to reveal the coloured wax underneath. Do it in a funky pattern!

7 Scrape your pattern along the page until you see your name revealed in a cool graffiti-style way!

How to draw a giraffe family with pastels

You will need: We've used oil pastels, but you can use chalk pastels or paints if you want

a piece of brown envelope paper

Now for something completely different – giraffes. These are lovely creatures and very simple to draw. We are using oil pastels – like chalk pastels, but slightly heavier, with a deeper colour.

Here's a basic outline for drawing a giraffe.

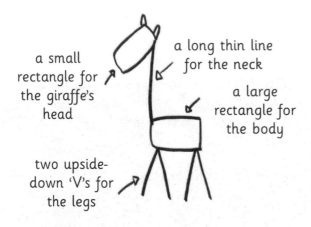

a small rectangle for the giraffe's head

a long thin line for the neck

a large rectangle for the body

two upside-down 'V's for the legs

❶ Draw a big zig-zag across your sheet of brown paper. Lightly shade it in with the same colour.

❷ Using a vibrant yellow, draw the basic outline of a large giraffe, and fill it in.

❸ Now add two baby giraffes, following behind.

4 Use the same yellow to draw a big sun in the sky and green to shade around the giraffes to make the grass.

5 Use brown to cover the giraffes' bodies with brown splodgy circles and then shade in the sky with blue.

6 Use the blue to go over the outline of the giraffes, carefully adding details like the tails, the eyes and the ears. Don't they look cute? You can almost feel the heat of the sun beating down on their backs.

How to draw a super steam train with pastels

Earlier in this book (on pages 56 and 57), you learned how to draw a simple picture of a moving truck using pastels. Here you can learn how to use pastels to create a much more detailed picture — this time we'll learn how to draw a moving steam train.

You will need:

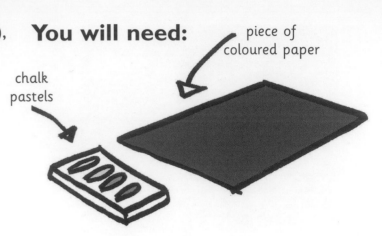

chalk pastels

piece of coloured paper

❶ Use a brown chalk pastel to draw a rough outline of your travelling train as shown.

❷ Pick a green chalk pastel and shade in the grass, using the side of the chalk instead of the pointed end.

❸ Shade parts of the sky blue then fill in the gaps with white chalk to make clouds. Use your finger to blend the two colours together where they meet.

❹ Draw some lights on the front of the train using a yellow pastel. Use the yellow to draw some windows on the carriages too.

5 Outline the front section of your train again using a darker brown or black. Use your thumb to smudge the chalk into the parts of the train you have outlined.

6 Do the same for the rest of the train. Add some smudges of black to the sky to make steam.

7 Now wash and dry your hands to get rid of the black. Take a purple chalk pastel and use it to outline the train again then smudge the colour into the body of the train as you did before. Add some white here and there, as shown.

8 Now outline the windows with a black chalk pastel, then use the black to go over a few other parts of your picture, like the big headlight.

Time to get going!

How to draw a monster truck using colouring pencils

Here's an artwork that will test you on the colouring pencil techniques you learned on page 24!

You will need:

piece of white paper

rubber

colouring pencils

❶ Using a dark blue or black colouring pencil, lightly draw the outline of an action scene. Try copying this monster truck – it's driving off a ramp into a ring of flames.

❷ Start shading the monster truck using the cross-hatching technique. Draw lots of little lines in opposite directions. Use yellow and orange for the circle of fire.

❸ Go around the flame using a bright red. Add fire to the back of the truck.

❹ Now shade the wheels with a black pencil. Use it to show the tread and texture of the tyres.

⑤ Now colour in the ground – we've used green, blue, brown and black.

⑥ Use a blue colouring pencil for the fence and black for the ramp.

⑦ Fill in the crowd by drawing lots of rough circles – put a smiley face on some of them. Colour in the rest of the picture then use your colours to go over the whole of the picture again to give it more texture. Then…take off!

How to make a city scene using black paper and colouring pencils

Colouring pencils are great because they work just as well on dark paper as they do on light paper. To illustrate this, let's create a bustling city by night.

You will need:

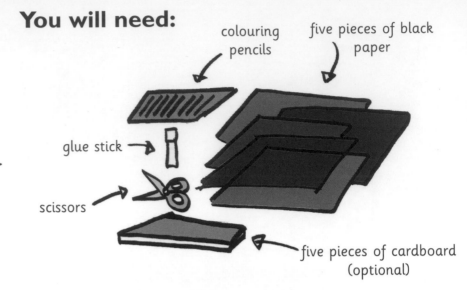

colouring pencils

five pieces of black paper

glue stick

scissors

five pieces of cardboard (optional)

❶ Take your five pieces of paper. On the first one, simply draw a moon at the top. Put this piece of paper to one side. Later we will stick the other layers on to this.

layer 1

❷ On your second piece of paper, draw a city skyline reaching about two-thirds up the paper. Cut round the skyline and then draw vague outlines of the buildings with a white pencil. Then add some shading with yellow and orange.

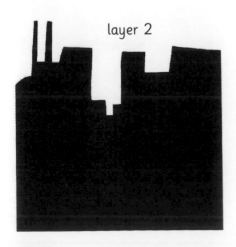

layer 2

❸ On the next piece of paper, draw a city horizon – a little shorter than the last layer. Cut it out. Then add the building's features in white. Colour the features however you want.

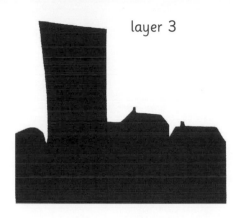

layer 3

❹ Follow the same procedure with the next piece, but this time the skyline should be shorter again. Remember – the closer the buildings, the more detail and colour they should have.

layer 4

❺ Now draw layer four. This has the most detail and is the shortest skyline.

❻ When you are happy with all four layers, you will be ready to stick them, one at a time, onto the first piece of paper which you have put to one side. Or, if you want to give the image more depth, you can stick each layer on to a piece of cardboard first. Then, when they are placed on top of each other, the depth will be exaggerated to create more of a 3D look.

How to create a snow scene using chalk pastels

You will need:

a piece of dark coloured paper

some chalk pastels

Chalk pastels give a lovely dusty, snowy effect. Use these illustrations on the right as a guideline for creating your brilliant snow scene.

the direction of the light source

where the darkest shadows will be

❶ Get your dark piece of paper and, using a light brown pastel, lightly sketch in the reindeer shape.

Use a white pastel to draw a faint circle in the top right-hand corner to remind us where the light is coming from. Then draw the basic shape of the snowman.

The different shadows will be in lots of different colours. We're going to use yellow, light brown, dark brown and purple for the reindeer, and white, blue and purple for the snowman.

Let's begin building up the image.

❷ Start with the highlights: the light brown and white.

❸ Then move on to the shadows: the purple.

❹ Fill in the main body of the reindeer. Go over the highlighted areas again, and then do the same with the shadows, so that there is a greater contrast.

❺ Finally, use a white pastel to create the falling snow with lots of dots and smudges.

How to paint a water scene using wax resistance

You will need:

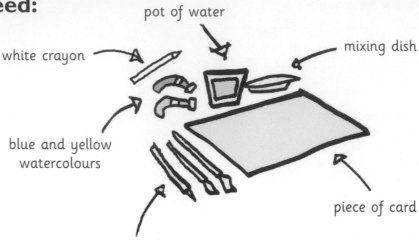

pot of water

white crayon

mixing dish

blue and yellow watercolours

piece of card

black pen and two brushes – one fat, one thin

❶ Decide on your image (such as a fish, an octopus, or whatever) and draw it using a black pen.

❷ Then take a white crayon and carefully draw in the detail such as scales, bubbles, etc.

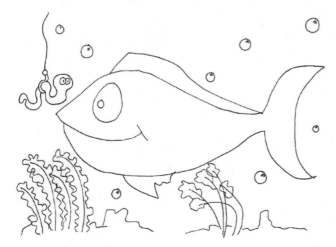

❸ Now take your blue watercolour paint. Mix it with a lot of water and paint over the whole page with your big paintbrush.

❹ Now, using the smaller paintbrush, mix the blue again but this time use a very small amount of water. Carefully go over your black pen lines.

❺ Still using the blue, paint in extra details, like more scales, and emphasize the plants.

❻ Finally, mix the yellow watercolour with some water (but don't make it too runny), and paint over the fish to give it a brilliant underwater feel.

How to paint a cat using batik

You will need:

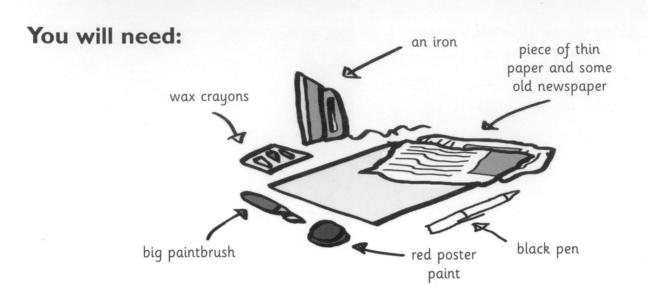

an iron

wax crayons

piece of thin paper and some old newspaper

big paintbrush

red poster paint

black pen

❶ Draw your image on the thin paper using a black pen.

❷ Get your wax crayons and colour in the picture. (You can't tell, but we've used white crayon in the white areas: this is a good colour to use as it stands out really well.)

❸ Carefully scrunch the picture into a ball. Try not to rip it!

❹ Un-scrunch it, then cover the whole picture with the red poster paint, using a big paintbrush. Wait until this is completely dry.

❺ Ask an adult to help you with the next step.

Switch the iron on, turning it to the cool setting. While it's heating up, get two sheets of old newspaper and put the painting in between them. Now iron the newspaper with your crumpled painting inside.

❻ You'll notice that the iron melts away the wax to reveal your picture underneath! The textured effect you get looks all crumpled and multi-coloured.

Using colour: summary

This chapter has introduced you to some really creative ways to make your artworks bright and bold.

To really get the most out of the top tips we've given you, you can use the techniques with different materials. Instead of using felt-tip pens to create a swirly lizard picture you could try using oil pastels instead.

You could even try using the long edges of chalk pastels to create a soft, bubbly underwater scene, using pages 72 and 73 as a guide.

If you're feeling ready to experiment with even more techniques and get really hands-on, turn to the next chapter and be creative!

Craft and Collage

How to paint an exotic bird using collage

Here's the first of our exciting craft projects in this chapter!

You will need:

acrylics or poster paints

pot of water

paintbrush

thick black pen

a piece of paper and an A4 piece of card

glue stick

❶ Get a piece of paper and paint lots of different colours on it. Make sure you include quite a few shades of green!

❷ Wait until it dries. Then rip the paper into little pieces. Sort the colours into different piles.

❸ Take all the bits of paper from your green pile and start to stick them on to a thick piece of A4 paper or card.

Continue until the whole page is covered. If you run out of green pieces just paint some more or rip up a picture of some green foliage from a magazine or newspaper.

4 When the glue has dried, take a thick black pen and roughly draw out the shape of your bird.

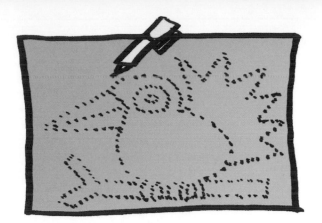

5 Use your yellow pieces of paper to make the beak. Use blue, orange and red pieces for the bird's body. Have fun using whatever colours you want for the tail feathers!

6 Finally, go over the outline of the bird again with your marker pen to complete the picture. Add the eye by cutting an oval shape of plain white paper and drawing on its beady eye!

How to build a space rocket using paper collage

You will need:

black card and coloured paper

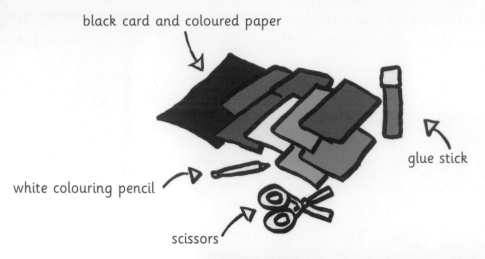

white colouring pencil

scissors

glue stick

❶ First of all, take your white colouring pencil and cover the black card with lots of little stars.

Then, using different coloured paper for each shape, cut out a rectangle, a triangle, and something that looks like a piece of toast! These are the main parts of your rocket.

❷ Now start to add on extra shapes to build up the image.

❸ To make flames, draw the three shapes on the right onto red, orange and yellow paper. Each one should be smaller than the one before. Cut them out and glue them on top of each other to give the appearance of flames.

④ To make the moon, cut out one big circle and one squished circle. Then cut out the middle of the squished circle to make a ring. Carefully slot the full circle into the ring and hey presto you have yourself a new planet!

⑤ Your space rocket should now be looking something like this.

⑥ Using thin strips and circles of coloured paper, build up the detail on the rocket and the moon. Blast off!

⑦ You can have fun making other pictures as well...

How to make a sunflower scene using tissue paper

You will need:

a pencil

a piece of paper and lots of tissue paper

glue stick

black ball-point or felt-tip pen

❶ First of all, sketch out your picture lightly in pencil.

❷ Now take the yellow tissue paper and rip out the rough shapes of the heads of the sunflowers. Stick these down with glue.

❸ Take the blue tissue paper and stick it down around the top edges. Don't worry if it's not neat.

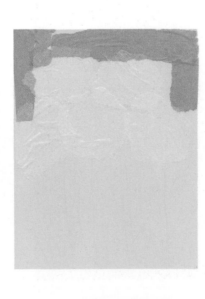

❹ Stick some green tissue paper in the bottom half of the picture. Now the whole page is filled with colour!

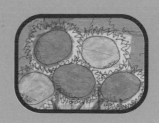

5 This is when you start to layer the colours. Add more orange and yellow to the centres of the sunflowers.

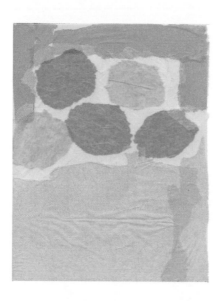

6 Now it's time to add the foliage. Rip up thin strips of green and stick them down.

7 Lastly, use your black pen to add the detail and outline your final shapes. Your sunflowers have been brought to life!

How to print spiky hedgehogs

You will need:

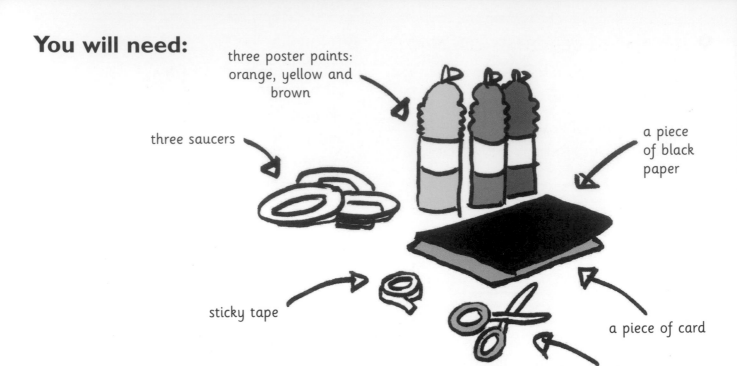

three poster paints:
orange, yellow and
brown

three saucers

a piece
of black
paper

sticky tape

a piece of card

scissors

Right, let's have some fun! For this picture we are going to print with paint. Printing is really cool because you never quite know how the paints are going to stick to the paper, so the effect is always a bit of a surprise!

Before we start, we have to make the printing blocks.

❶ Take your card and draw three different sized triangles. (You can draw them by hand or use a ruler – it's up to you.) Then cut them out with scissors. These triangles are your printing blocks.

❷ Put your triangles to one side. Now cut three strips (about one centimetre/half an inch wide) out of the leftover card. These strips will act as handles for your printing blocks.

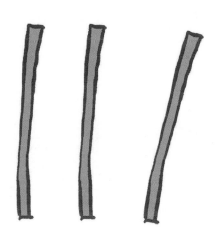

❸ To make the handles, fold each strip in half. Then bend the ends upwards to make little flaps. Attach a handle to each triangle by sticking down the flaps with sticky tape.

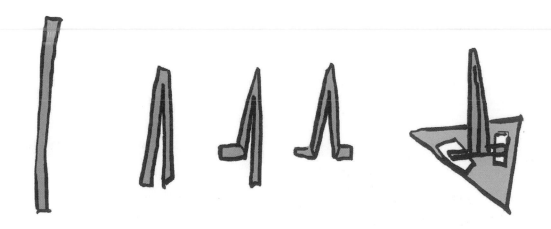

❹ Now pour each of your poster paints into a separate saucer, so you have a yellow saucer, an orange saucer and a brown saucer. Great. You're ready to begin!

❺ Dunk your biggest printing block into the orange paint. Now firmly press down in the bottom left-hand corner of your page.

❻ Now get the medium-sized printing block and dunk it in the brown paint. Print several triangles in an arc as shown.

❼ Pick up your smallest printing block, dunk it in the yellow saucer and print a smaller arc of triangles beneath the brown triangles.

follow this pattern

❽ Pick up the medium-sized block again and dunk it first into the brown saucer, then lightly in the orange. Print a third arc.

❾ Again, dunk the small triangle into the yellow and print another arc.

❿ We finished off with the brown medium-sized block, but you could go on and on! To complete the picture, add the hedgehog's eye by dunking your little finger in the brown saucer and press down where you want the eye to be!

How to paint a colliding truck

We think you'll really enjoy these pages. We'll show you how to turn a moving truck into a collision scene! You can do all this on one piece of paper, too.

You will need:

poster paints

pot of water

thick card or paper

pencil and paintbrush

ruler

the dotted lines divide the paper into three equal sections

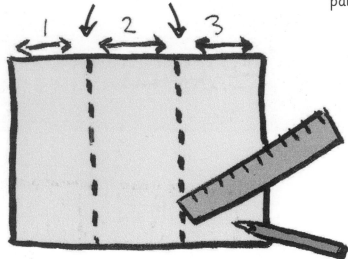

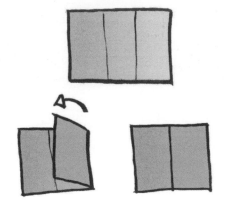

❶ Measure the long side of your piece of paper then divide this by three. Draw two dotted lines in pencil to mark the three equal sections. Later you will be folding the paper along these lines. Turn the paper over so the lines are on the back.

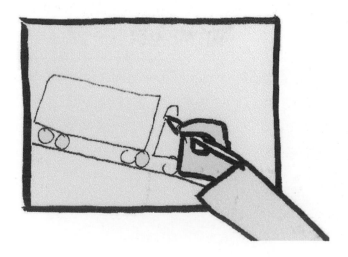

❷ With the blank side facing upwards, use a pencil to draw the crash scene you can see on the opposite page. Draw your truck on a sloping line so it looks like it is speeding downhill. Make sure the truck stretches across more than half of your piece of paper. (Check by looking at the dotted lines on the back.) Draw one of the car wheels up in the air and add some dramatic zig-zag shapes too.

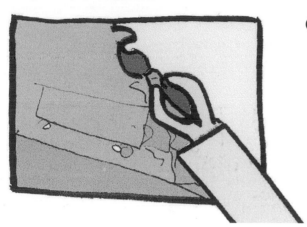

3 Next, use your poster paints to make your picture as bold and bright as possible. You can copy the colours in the picture below if you like.

4 Your finished picture should look a bit like this. Use a dark blue or black for the background to make it seem as if it's the middle of the night.

5 Wait for your painting to dry then fold the right-hand third of the page inwards, along the second dotted line you drew earlier. This should cover up the damaged part of your truck, as well as the car. Now turn to the next page of this book to find out how to fix your truck!

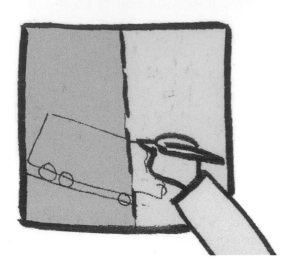

6 On the white part of your folded piece of paper, draw the front section of your truck again. This time the truck should be driving along the road in perfect condition! The picture below should help you to draw it. Make sure your truck's new front section lines up with the back part of the truck that you drew before.

7 Now you're ready to paint your new drawing. Use exactly the same colours as you used before so that the two sides of your new scene match to make one perfect picture.

8 To show movement, paint some white lines in the sky above the front of your truck and around the front wheels.

9 Wait for the paint to dry then see how your picture of the truck unfolds...

10 ...to reveal a wreck!

How to create a colourful fire engine collage

Collages get you to think about all the different shapes that make up one picture. Make sure you draw each shape in pencil first before you try to cut it out.

This fire engine collage will look best on a piece of black paper.

You will need:

coloured paper

glue

scissors

pencil

❶ Cut out a windscreen shape from white paper and a bonnet shape from red paper. Stick the shapes down.

❷ Make a sausage-shaped bumper using some grey paper and the roof from some red paper.

❸ Make the engine grill and some small rectangles for wing mirrors from grey paper. Use blue paper for the tyres.

❹ Make lights from small circles of yellow paper. Cut some in half for the top lights.

❺ Build up flame shapes in layers of different colours.

red   orange   yellow   white   =   multi-coloured flame

❻ Draw a zig-zag shape on a piece of red paper and cut out the middle part. Draw a larger zig-zag shape on blue paper and cut it out. The red and blue shapes form the border for your picture.

❼ Stick the red frame down on your picture then stick the blue frame down on top of that.

❽ Add some thin shapes round the headlights to make them dazzle!

How to paint a boat using only tissue paper!

You will need:

pencil

black paint or felt-tip pen

pot of water

scissors

two pieces of paper and lots of tissue paper

paintbrush

Did you ever think that you could paint with tissue paper? Well you can! This is how:

❶ First of all, take a piece of paper and draw a rough outline of what you are going to paint. This will act as a useful guide.

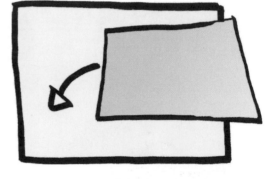

❷ Then cut out a big rectangle of blue tissue paper. This will be the background colour. Place it on the second, clean piece of paper.

❸ Get a paintbrush, wet it, and brush the water over the tissue paper. Make sure that it is completely covered.

❹ Now carefully pull the tissue paper off. There will be a blue rectangular print of colour left on the page! Wow!

5 Now do the same with the boat. Take some brown tissue paper, cut out the shape and position it on your piece of paper. Wet the tissue paper using your paintbrush again. Then peel off.

Do exactly the same thing with the sails (which are just two triangles). Then do the sun (a yellow circle) and the anchor.

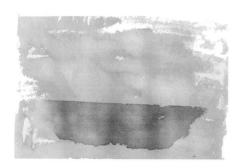  

6 Finally, use a black felt-tip or some black paint to outline the edges. This helps to make the picture look stronger, but you don't have to do it if you don't want to.

How to make greetings cards

You will need:

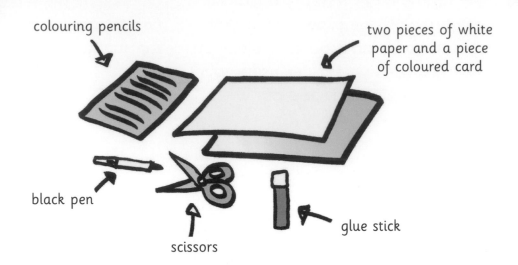

colouring pencils

two pieces of white paper and a piece of coloured card

black pen

scissors

glue stick

This is a really easy yet impressive way to make cards for your family and friends!

❶ Take your plain piece of paper and draw four small boxes in black ball-point or felt-tip. Inside the boxes draw pictures that are suitable for the occasion. For example, we're making a greetings card for our niece's first birthday, so we have drawn a pram, some building blocks, a cake and a rocking horse.

Colour in the black and white drawings with your colouring pencils. Use scissors to cut out the square.

❷ Now pick up your piece of coloured card and carefully fold it in half. Position it so that it opens on the right-hand side.

3 Stick your square of pictures onto the front of the coloured card with some glue.

4 On the second piece of white paper, write the message that you want to say (we've put, 'Happy 1st Birthday' on ours). Colour it in, cut it out, and stick it at the top of your card.

Hey presto! Easy, quick cards that look great!

Here are some more cards you could make:

How to make a mermaid place mat

You will need:

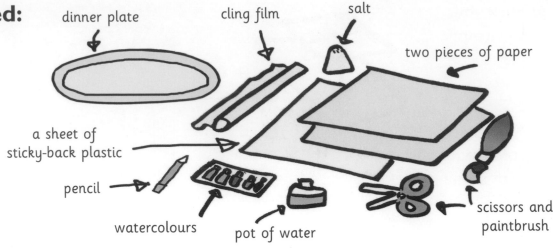

dinner plate

cling film

salt

two pieces of paper

a sheet of sticky-back plastic

pencil

watercolours

pot of water

scissors and paintbrush

❶ Draw the basic shape of your mermaid faintly in pencil.

❷ Start filling in the skin with a pale flesh colour from your watercolours.

❸ Paint the whole tail with yellow, adding some red and orange while it's wet. Sprinkle some salt over the tail.

❹ When the paint and salt are dry, brush the salt off. The tail has scales!

❺ Paint the hair in brown. Then use some red for the bikini top.

❻ Wait until all the paint has dried, then cut the mermaid out.

7 Take your other piece of paper and wet it with your brush before painting it blue. Take some cling film from the kitchen and put it over the wet piece of paper.

8 Keep it there until the paint has dried. When you take the cling film off, you will see that it has left an amazing watery pattern!

9 Put a dinner plate on your blue page and draw round it. Remove the plate and use the drawn circle as a guide to cut out the shape of your place mat.

10 Put the mermaid on the blue circle. Place a sheet of sticky-back plastic over the top, cut round the edges. Hooray! You have yourself a mermaid place mat! To make it even more fancy, you could try mounting it on thick cardboard or even some cork tiling.

Craft and collage: summary

This chapter has introduced you to some really creative ways to make artworks and personalised gifts. While we've shown you how to use tissue paper, card and paint, you can let your imagination run wild and use whatever materials you can get your hands on!

Try painting the spiky hedgehogs (page 84) using potato blocks instead of card. Remember to ask an adult to help you cut them out, though.

You could even try creating an environmentally-friendly collage by recycling old sweet wrappers, coloured cardboard and any other brightly coloured things you can find. A recycled rocket (page 80) would be out of this world!

How to Paint

How to paint a flower using mixed watercolours

You will need:

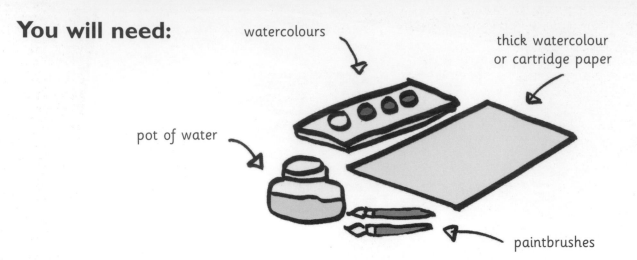

watercolours

thick watercolour or cartridge paper

pot of water

paintbrushes

❶ We'll start this chapter with watercolours. The fantastic thing about watercolours is the way that you can make so many wonderful shades just by mixing a few colours. As you can see with the painting of the flower (opposite), you can produce loads of different hues when you apply wet colour on to more wet colour.

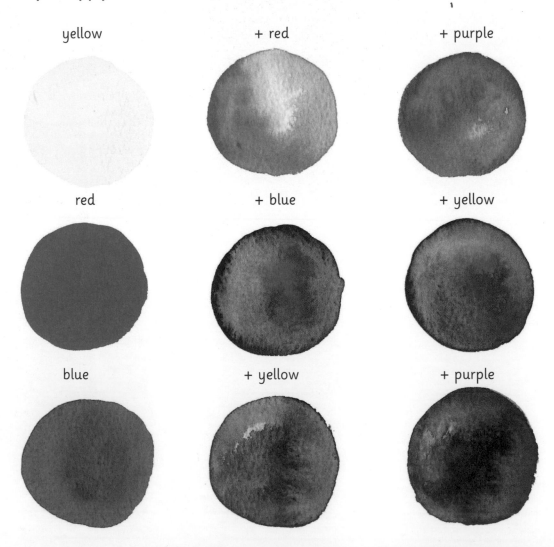

yellow	+ red	+ purple
red	+ blue	+ yellow
blue	+ yellow	+ purple

2 Simply decide on your base colour (we've used yellow here) and paint it on to your page, making sure that it is quite watery. Immediately add another colour to your wet paint, and then another, and so on. The effect is a kaleidoscope of colours and shades. This technique is very handy when you want to paint something that has a large tonal range.

you need to leave gaps when applying wet colour onto wet colour. Otherwise all the colours would run across the whole petal

the centre of the flower is yellow plus red plus purple

the base shade is yellow. Then add light red

start off with yellow. Then add blue and green

again, start off with yellow. Then add orange and brown

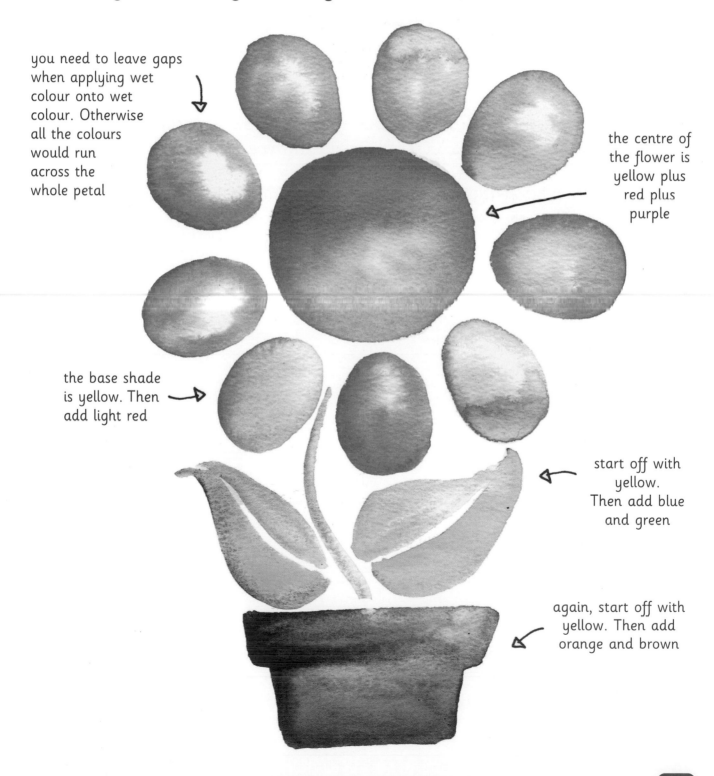

How to paint a monkey scene using gouache

You will need:

gouache paints

pot of water

sheet of white paper

paintbrush and pencil

Earlier (page 50) we looked at how to draw monkeys. Now we'll try painting them! Gouache paints give a nice flat colour, but any type of paint will do.

❶ Draw your monkey jungle scene. Fill the page with lots of leaves, vines and branches.

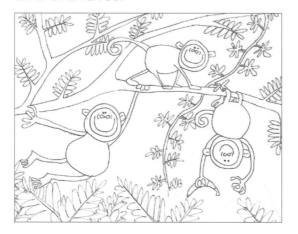

❷ Paint the background with a light green, taking care not to paint over any lines.

❸ Use a light brown and paint the branches.

❹ Choose shades of green and brown for the leaves and vines.

❺ When you're happy with the background, start on the monkeys. We coloured their bodies with a thick dark brown. It makes them stand out from the background.

❻ For the faces you want to use a flesh-coloured paint. If you can't find one, mix some white with some brown and a tiny bit of pink.

❼ When the faces are dry, use the point of your paintbrush to and carefully paint in the mouth, nose and eyes on each of the monkeys. If you don't have a fine enough paintbrush, a pen or colouring pencil will do.

How to paint a monster using acrylics

You will need:

acrylics

pot of water

piece of paper

paintbrushes and pencil

❶ The wonderful thing about acrylic paint is that you can have fun making marks in the paint while it's still wet. Also, because it's so thick, it's really easy to add lots of colours on top of each other without ending up with a smudgy mess!

❷ We're going to use acrylics to paint a monster. Start by drawing the monster's body in pencil. Apply a thick layer of blue acrylic. While it's still wet, use the end of the brush to make little lines in the paint. These will be white because the paper underneath is showing through.

❸ Next, paint the arms, legs, eyes and mouth in bright yellow. Again, this will be easier if you draw them out lightly in pencil first.

4 Now fill in the background with red. When it is dry, take some white paint and cover the background in white spots. Acrylic is the only paint that lets you do this – that's why it's so much fun! You can add as many colours on top of each other as you want.

5 Finally, use black to finish off the eyes and add any last-minute details that you want (like the blue dots on the white spots).

How to paint a near and far landscape using oil paints

You will need:

In this art project, we're going to to learn about painting a landscape. Unlike the watercolour project on page 22, here we'll be using oil paints and three pieces of paper to add more depth.

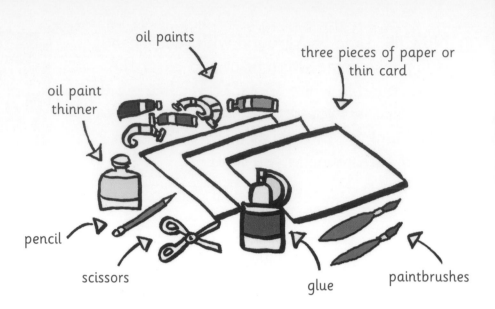

oil paints

three pieces of paper or thin card

oil paint thinner

pencil

scissors

glue

paintbrushes

1 On the first piece of paper, paint the sky and far away hills. This should not contain much detail.

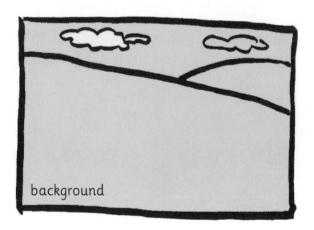

background

2 On the second piece, paint closer, smaller hills with a few trees on them. This should have a bit more detail. When the painting is dry, cut it out.

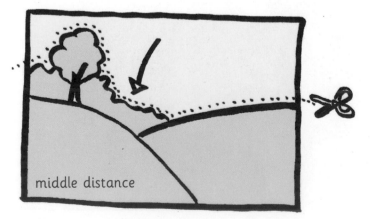

middle distance

❸ On the third and final piece of paper, paint a close up of a hill with an animal or some flowers on it. We have added some sheep. This sheet should contain the biggest, most detailed images. Cut it out when it is dry.

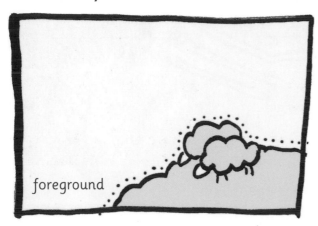

foreground

❹ Now place your two cut-outs on to your background. Immediately the painting has depth and perspective. It's a tricky technique made simple!

placing the 3 layers together creates depth

not much detail in the background

add different colour and texture to each hill

you have the closest image at the front of the picture

How to paint creepy crawlies

You will need:

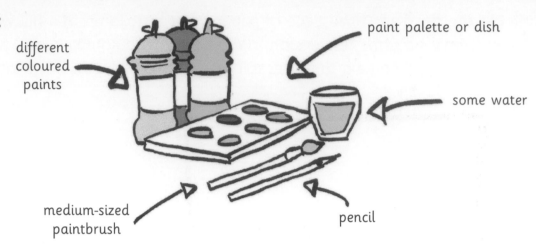

different coloured paints

paint palette or dish

some water

medium-sized paintbrush

pencil

We're going to paint something very simple – a snail! The great thing about a snail is that it can be drawn in about five seconds and it's very easy to do.

❶ Begin with the shell. Start in the middle and paint one long spiralling circle.

❷ Next comes the body. It looks like a pointy sausage.

❸ Finally, we need to add the antennae. These are achieved by drawing a large capital 'V'.

Now that you have drawn the basic shape, you can have lots of fun deciding how to decorate the shell. Here are some examples:

a spotted shell

a striped shell

a colour-filled shell

Once you've mastered the technique, you can use it as the starting point for many other creepy crawlies...

to make a wood louse, take away the shell and add lots of tiny legs to each side of the body

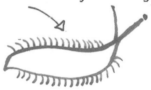

a slug is so easy: just take away the shell from a snail. Ta da!

to make a butterfly, don't take away the shell, but add another one to the other side

then add two smaller ones at the bottom

How to paint a swirly colour cat

You will need:

Like the sunflowers on page 102, we're going to mix watercolours together. This time, the colours will all run together to give a soft, cuddly effect. Perfect for a cat!

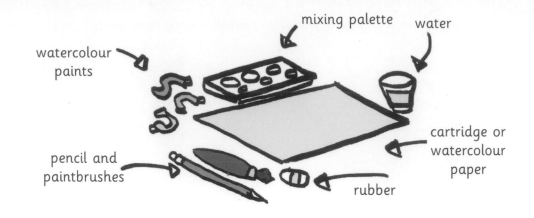

watercolour paints

mixing palette

water

pencil and paintbrushes

cartridge or watercolour paper

rubber

❶ Take your paper and draw the rough outline of a cat.

❷ Rub out the pencil marks where the different body parts join together.

❸ Now dip your paintbrush in water and 'paint' the inside of your cat. Only with water, though!

❹ Use yellow paint to go over some of the wet paper. Then use some red to paint over the remaining area. You will see the two paints blend together to make lots of gorgeous colours.

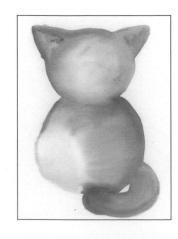

5 'Paint' around the cat with clean water, but leave a space around him so that the colours inside and outside don't mix.

6 Go over the water with some blue paint.

7 Then paint over again with some green and yellow paint.

8 Wait until the paint is completely dry, then finish off by adding in the face and whiskers with brown paint. Purrfect!

How to paint a porky piggy with oil paints

You will need:

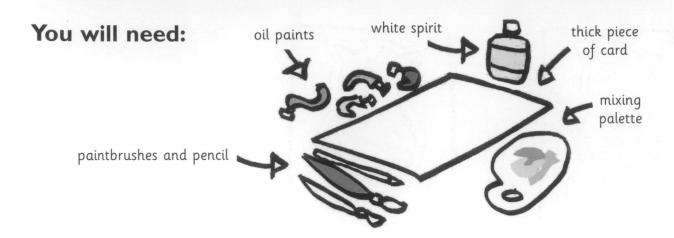

oil paints

white spirit

thick piece of card

mixing palette

paintbrushes and pencil

❶ With a pencil, draw a big friendly pig on to a thick piece of card.

❷ Paint the background with a large brush. Include as many different shades of green, yellow and blue as you want.

❸ Mix together some orange and pink and use a smaller brush to fill in the body. A bit of yellow will perk up his bottom a bit!

❹ Use pink and orange for your pig's face.

5 Add a bit of brown to your flesh-coloured paint and mix until you're happy with the shade. Then paint in the nose and the back pair of legs and trotters.

6 It's time for the nostrils! They are an even darker shade, so add some more brown to the mix and paint in the massive circles.

7 Using the brown on its own, put a small amount on a clean dry brush and dab a few circles on top of the pig's body to give him big, piggy freckles. Lastly, use a dark brown or black to paint in the eyes. You have to remember to paint in his wonderful corkscrew tail, too!

How to paint a train travelling through the mountains

You can make this colourful scene using just four paints – blue, red, yellow and white. See the colour charts on pages 16 and 17 if you need a reminder about mixing primary colours.

You will need:

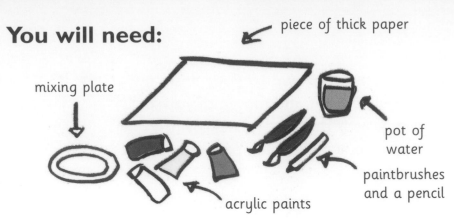

piece of thick paper

mixing plate

pot of water

paintbrushes and a pencil

acrylic paints

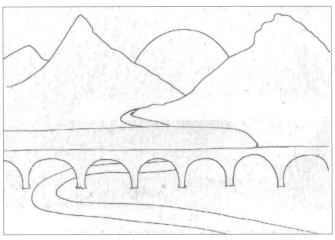

❶ First, draw your picture in pencil. Don't forget the train!

❷ Mix blue and yellow paints together to paint the grass a nice green colour.

❸ Add a bit more blue to the green to make a darker shade. Use it to start painting the mountain on the right, working from the bottom up. As you get nearer the top, add some white to the paint to make it lighter.

❹ Now paint the mountain to the left of the sun. It should be paler than the mountain on the right as this will make it look further away. Make the mountain behind it even paler. Then mix some yellow with a tiny amount of red to paint the sun.

5 Next get ready to paint the sky. Add a lot of red to some yellow paint, then add a little bit of white – this will make the sky look misty. What a spectacular sunset!

6 Mix some blue paint with a little bit of white to paint the river. Start at the bottom of your picture and add more white to the paint as you go along. Next mix blue, yellow and red to paint the bridge brown.

7 Carefully paint a blue stripe on the train then wait for this to dry. Now add some white to your blue paint. Using your smallest paintbrush, paint some little rectangles and lines on the train to make windows and doors. Zoom!

How to paint a psychedelic elephant

You will need: poster paints, watercolours or acrylics (whatever you like!)

glass of water

a piece of thick paper or card

a paintbrush and a pencil

The good thing about elephants is that they are so big. So when painting an elephant you can have lots of fun filling the body and head with weird and wacky colours and markings. You don't have to strictly follow what we've done. Just use your imagination to think of cool and exciting patterns!

❶ First draw your elephant in pencil. (Have a look at page 44 if you need to.)

❷ Now fill the elephant's body with lots of stars.

❸ Use your yellow paint to colour in the spaces around the stars.

❹ Clean your paintbrush, fill it with red paint and colour in the stars.

❺ Now it's time for the ears. We've chosen to do semi-circles within semi-circles, but you could do whatever you fancy. Use a pencil before painting the pattern if it's a bit tricky.

❻ We decided to cover the elephant's head with lots of tiny circles and fill the trunk with bigger and bigger arrows.

Turn to the next page to see how to finish the psychedelic elephant!

Finishing the psychedelic elephant

7 We painted the elephant's head with orange, leaving the little circles clear. After a bit of thought, we decided to paint these circles yellow. Last of all, the trunk was painted with alternate colours of orange and yellow.

8 You could stop here, but it's much more fun to carry on! With a clean brush, take some blue paint and dot your way round the outline of the elephant. Once you've gone the entire way round, do it again!

9 Now take some lighter blue or green and go around the elephant again and again, changing the colour of paint whenever you want, until you have filled the page with colourful dots. Then get a black pen, or put some black paint on your brush, and go round the outline of the elephant.

10 To finish the piece, clean your brush and cover it with orange paint.
With the tip of the brush, paint some dots in any spaces left over.
Last of all, paint a big orange border around the edges of the paper.
See if you can paint a wackier elephant than the one we've done!

How to spot paint using acrylics

You will need:

Spot painting is a great technique. It gives your pictures a new twist and is fun and easy to do.

acrylic paints

a palette

piece of paper

glass of water

a fat brush, a thin brush and a pencil

❶ Draw out your tortoise in pencil, then use your big paintbrush to paint some flat areas of colour.

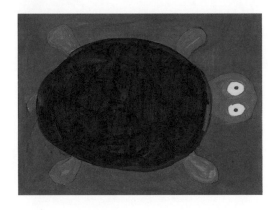

❷ Now take your smaller paintbrush and dip it into a bright yellow paint. Very lightly, paint dots of colour around the shape of the tortoise.

❸ Your picture should now look like the one below.

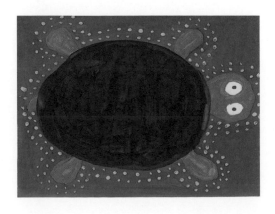

4 Once you have gone round the tortoise a few times, change the colour of the spots to orange or red. Continue to do this until the whole background is covered.

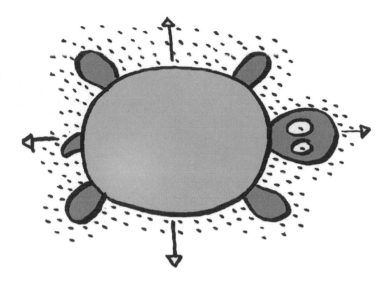

5 Now move on to the shell. Paint your spots in a winding circular pattern, so that they look like mini whirlpools. Do lots and lots of these different coloured whirlpools until the shell is full.

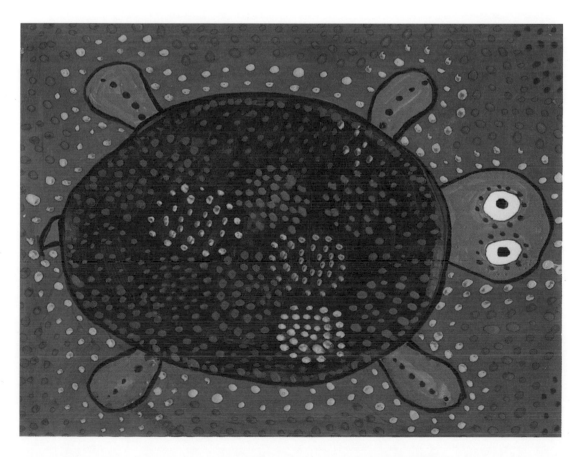

6 Finally, add extra spots to any other places that might need them, such as around the eyes.

How to paint the Loch Ness monster using watercolours

You will need:

watercolours

thick watercolour or cartridge paper

pot of water

paintbrushes

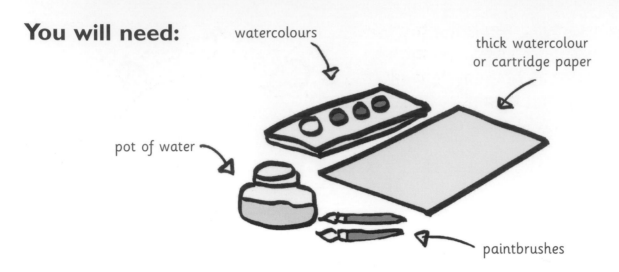

❶ Let's start with the water. First, wet the area that you want to paint before going over it again with the blue colour. This way you can easily add different shades of blue to the lake, giving it depth.

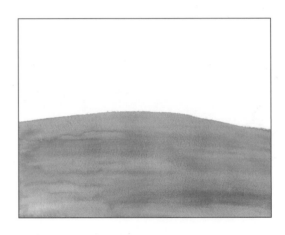

❷

To paint the sky, do the same thing: wet the area first and then go over it with watercolour. Leave a zig-zag space for the mountains. To make really good cloud shapes, you could get a tissue, scrunch it up in your hand, and dab at the wet blue sky.

❸ Now take your green paint and fill in the mountains. Remember that the further away they are, the lighter green you should use.

4 Making sure that the lake is dry, take your paintbrush and dip it into some strong yellowy-white paint. Don't add too much water, as you want the paint to be really thick. Now paint in three arcs, a long wiggly neck and a head.

5 When that has dried, add a tiny bit of brown to the watercolour mixture and go over the monster again.

6 Finally, take a thin paintbrush, mix up a strong brown colour, and go around the outline of your Loch Ness monster. Then add his mouth and eyes. You might even like to paint on some scales – this is done by painting lots of little 'u's on his body.

How to paint a sheep scene with cotton buds

You will need:

any kind of paints

coloured paper

black pen

glue

scissors

saucer

cotton buds

A useful thing to remember about paint is that you don't always have to use a paintbrush to create a picture. To finish off this chapter, we're going to show you how to use cotton buds instead!

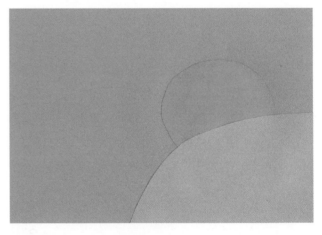

❶ First of all we need to make a collage background. Start by taking your scissors, cutting out a yellow circle, and sticking it down on a sheet of blue paper.

❷ Take some green paper and cut out a little hill. Use your glue to stick it onto the bottom right-hand corner of your page so that it just overlaps your sun.

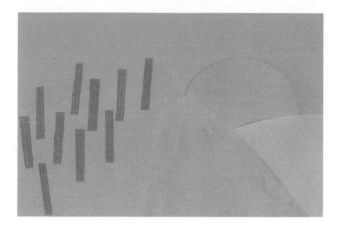

❸ Now cut a larger green hill and stick it down onto the bottom left-hand corner of your page.

❹ Use a brown envelope to cut up about ten small tree trunks and stick them on as shown above.

❺ Using yellow paper, cut out some rays for your sun. Stick these down and then it's time to start painting!

Put a blob of the pale and dark green paints on the side of the saucer. Dip a cotton bud into the pale green paint, then dab at the top of a tree trunk. Build it up until you have a big round circle of cotton bud blobs. Then get a fresh cotton bud and do the same with the dark green paint until you have covered all the tree trunks.

❻ Now get some white paint, squirt a blob onto the saucer, and use a cotton bud to paint the sheep on the hill. They should look like lots of little white fluffy clouds.

Turn to the next page to learn how to finish the scene!

Finishing the cotton bud sheep scene

7 Add a dab of blue to the white paint on your saucer. Mix them to create a bluey-white colour. With a fresh cotton bud, paint some long wispy clouds over the sun and sky.

8 This part is very simple. Use some yellow paint to create a polka dot effect over the back hill.

9 Finally, using either some black paint or a marker pen, draw in the sheep's stick legs and oval heads. There you have it – your own fluffy cotton bud scene! Try it with bears, cats and any other furry animals you can think of!